CANON FOR BEARS
AND PONDEROSA PINES

Poems by
Diane Frank

GLASS LYRE PRESS

Copyright © 2018 Diane Frank
Paperback ISBN: 978-1-941783-44-3

All rights reserved: except for the purpose of quoting brief passages for review, no part of this book may be reproduced or transmitted in any form or by any means, electronic or mechanical, including photocopying, recording, or by any information storage and retrieval system, without permission in writing from the publisher.

Cover art: © Venantius J Pinto
Design & layout: Steven Asmussen

Glass Lyre Press, LLC
P.O. Box 2693
Glenview, IL 60025
www.GlassLyrePress.com

Acknowledgments

Deep appreciation to Ami Kaye of Glass Lyre Press, for her vision, her poetry, and her desire to publish this book.

"Margalit" won First Prize in the 2017 Dancing Poetry Contest and was published in *The Art of Awe and the Power of Your Artist's Statement*, by Natica Angilly.

Grateful acknowledgment to the following magazines and anthologies in which some of these poems were previously published: *Pirene's Fountain: Silk and Spice, Miramar #5, Poetry Breakfast, Haight Ashbury Literary Journal, Cyclamens and Swords, PoetryBay, The Long Islander, Vista and Byways, Cloudbank 11, Allegro & Adagio, Eternal Snow, Conch.es, sisterfrombelow.com, Suddenly the Earth is Singing, Painting the Eucalyptus Midnight,* and *Earth Music.*

Praise for Canon for Bears & Ponderosa Pines

"In this new and startling collection, Diane Frank's poems transcend not just genres but entire dimensions. When she speaks to J.S. Bach, she really means it and when Bach speaks back, she listens – entirely – the way certain moths perceive sound via their whole body, even their wings. How is this accomplished? It will seem to come through the poems themselves – their music, tonal qualities and subjects, yet it goes even deeper as it pushes up like *duende* through the soles of your feet. The voice is declarative, emphatic, spirit driven. She will tell you, '*When a buffalo enters your dream, / listen for arpeggio hooves, / the weight of music, / a copper moon / above a vanishing prairie*' and you will, you must listen."

–**Lois P. Jones,** author of *Night Ladder*
Radio Host, KPFK's *Poets Café*

"*Canon for Bears and Ponderosa Pines* is a feast for the senses, the images conjuring sights, sounds and tastes that metamorphosize into larger concepts. However, when Diane Frank introduces music into her poetry, it takes on a depth, both joyful and painful, that is, in my opinion, her finest work. Bravo!"

–**Jill Rachuy Brindel**
Cellist, San Francisco Symphony

"In Diane Frank's *Canon for Bears and Ponderosa Pines,* this reader finds himself embraced by trees. While hiking in Muir Woods, the poet sees, 'Lichens and gnomes / in the bark of giant redwoods, / ribbons of brown and pink, / striations remembered from earlier times.' Diane Frank's observations link us with the essence of life, with earth. We are penetrated by a music we can both hear and see. The sensuousness of life is accentuated in dances we feel from our most primal bodily memories."

–**Rustin Larson,** author of *Pavement*,
Winner of the 2016 Blue Light Poetry Prize

"How deep is the music of the spheres locked up inside our earthly, material existence? So deep, says Diane Frank, that it could take a lifetime 'to learn the cello's toning to what I hear.' So close to the surface that it's present in the sound of icefall or a mountain bird drunk with song.

In *Canon for Bears and Ponderosa Pines,* she takes us on a journey to unlock that music for her readers – to make the 'impossible note' manifest. In these resonant poems, she takes us to the deep hidden places, and to the transparently spellbinding surfaces – in search of that 'music or soundscape, rising like a flood.' The journey is sacred and profane – from the arpeggio of buffalo hooves to the cacophony of an alarm in a high school classroom during a bomb scare. And through her poetry, the line between sacred and profane is erased, and what emerges is the music within. What does she discover in a field of ice wrapped trees? An ocean of violins. In redwoods, and the long fingers of ferns? Water music. What does she discover in a purple balloon held in a small child's hand? Hearts filled with musical joy.

Open this book. Listen for the impossible note, for the musical stuff that binds everything. Before very long, you're likely to discover, as Diane Frank has, that it's everywhere – as resonant as the way a string vibrates at the intersection of bow and memory."

–George Wallace
Writer in Residence at the Walt Whitman Birthplace

"Diane Frank is a magician, flying on a cello, wearing black slinky pants. She walks like a geisha, with a paper umbrella, unless of course she is riding a tortoise. Buffalos dance out of Beethoven's arpeggios, with their hooves. Diane Frank invites you into her dream – *Canon for Bears and Ponderosa Pines,* where a thousand Swiss cows clang their bells for you in the moonlight. Don't expect to read this collection of poems and remain unmoved. You cannot easily wash away the scent of bear, honey, topaz blue light."

–Midwife Robin Lim, Bali, Indonesia
Author of *The Geometry of Splitting Souls*

"Diane Frank's new book, *Canon for Bears and Ponderosa Pines,* invites us to transcend and be transformed by an ecstatic engagement with the natural world – each poem a lush, primordial garden of flora and fauna, overlaid with the omnipresent music of the spheres. There is mystery and surprise with every turn of the page here, lighting up our senses and perceptions with poems not just inspired by natural and symphonic music, but invoked and informed by it. From the poem "Pentagram: Garden Walk," we read: 'Love is a whir of hummingbirds, / an open window, / a garden of passion flowers and wild orchids, / indigo butterflies mating in a kaleidoscope of wings, / a memory, a dream you suddenly remember.' Like Diane Frank's previous books, this one does not disappoint, enchanting us with its sensual imagery and rhythms. As Kim Addonizio writes, "Poetry is not a means to an end, but a continuing engagement with being alive." After finishing *Canon for Bears and Ponderosa Pines,* you will no doubt feel more alive than when you picked it up."

–**Christopher Seid**, *Author of Age of Exploration*

"To be inside these poems is to feel the warmth of the sun after a violent storm, illuminating the way for a mermaid to swim through an O'Keeffe cow skull, with a guide book of wildflowers and a shaman's drum, singing the heartbeat rhythms of incarnation and ancestry, listening to life as music, the goose-flesh eroticism of nature's ceaseless rhythms, an interpenetrating dream with the shivering overtones of truth, like stars, the tides, the hunger of the ants that allows the peonies to blossom. Dickinson said, 'If I feel physically as if the top of my head were taken off, I know that is poetry.' This is what happens when one encounters the Rumi-meets-Alice in Wonderland *duende* of Diane Frank."

–**David Hurlin**, Author of *Zero Gravity Funk Libido*

Contents

Acknowledgments — iii

Dreams of the Ecliptic — 1
Margalit — 2
Just Between — 4
Virtuoso — 5
Cello Lesson — 8
Magnificat — 10
Ultra-Body Over the Mountain — 12
Earthquake, 5 A.M. — 14
Blackbird, Plum, Ripple — 15
What Your Cat Did During Your
    Vacation at the Grand Canyon — 16
Under a Copper Moon — 17
Canon for Bears and Ponderosa Pines — 18
Igneous — 20
Jar with Dragons — 22
Music of the Spheres — 24
Photographs of the Pleasure Quarter — 25
Ice Field — 27
Orb — 30
Joy, like a Purple Balloon — 31
Best Day Ever — 32
Garden Buddha — 34
Embraced by Trees — 35
Fire Walk — 37
Ferry Boat to the Moon — 38
Catalina Island — 40

Where it Comes From	41
Intermezzo	42
Picasso's Dream	43
Pentagram: Garden Walk	44
Transmigration	46
The Open Book of Riddles	47
Kaleidoscope	48
October Secret	49
A Ruby in his Beard	50
While Listening to the Quartet for Piano and Strings by Tom Darter	51
Moon Blizzard, Saxophone Dream	53
Packing Up George	55
Six Months in Arosa	58
When you fly . . .	60
Zoo Story	61
Hemiola	62
Twin Dreams	63
After the End of the Road	66
Hidden Variables	68
Ode to New Music	70
Miso Soup	71
Puberty	72
Invisible Ink Picnic	74
Asphalt Impressionism	76
Owl, Dream, Mountain	77
Sunset over the Pacific	78
Planting Tulips	79
Morning Meditation	80
Two Sunsets	82
Jumping A Train	84
About the Author	87

Dreams of the Ecliptic

To change a girl into a kite,
    tell her that love is the moon.

To teach a tree to sing,
    put a harp under its branches.

To change a bowl of dust into a planet,
    paint watercolor rings around the ecliptic.

To change the sky into a dream,
    put a song into a hammock.

To melt an ice cube,
    light a fire under the map of the constellations.

To write a symphony in a major key,
    plant a rainbow under an apple tree.

To create a universe,
    ride on a meteor shower
        as the archer shoots a path of light
        across the sky.

When the sun rises for the first time,
    fill the sky with your singing.

Margalit

For Margalit Oved, Yemenite dancer and choreographer

"The *duende* surges up from the soles of the feet...
It is not a matter of ability but of real, live form;
of blood; of ancient culture."
–Federico Garcia Lorca, *Theory and Function of the Duende*

The younger dancer didn't have what she did –
the swaying of eucalyptus leaves in her fingers,
the taste of old world salt on her breath.
Margalit was like the flamenco dancer
with fire in her throat,
hibiscus on her lips,
belly swaying in the rhythm of the sea.

Yes, I know. . .
The violist who stopped performing
before the arc of his vibrato
passed its prime. The french horn player
who eased himself out of the opera
while his lips still had the ability to kiss his wife.
The ballerina who set up a dance academy
after her swan song.

Margalit said her protege
could execute subtle moves that her aging body
did not have the agility to perform,
but this is what I saw –
a young tree with hollow branches,
the flaming red and burnt umber
of the change of season
absent from her pallet of painting oils.
Her movements lithe but lacking *duende*,
too much sunshine in her hands.

I wanted to feel
the spice of black olives in a Yemenite market,
the cucumbers and tomatoes,
the drum made from the recycled tin
that was filled with olive oil.
I wanted to feel the rhythm
of long boats pulling fish from the Mediterranean sea,
the nets of the fishermen.
I wanted to watch her veined and beautiful hands
gathering rosebuds from her mother's garden,
brass bells dreaming on her ankles
with the memory of the land where she was born,
and the way her mother carried her across the desert
to the Promised Land.

Just Between

I tossed an Egyptian moth
in front of his eye. In the morning,
it hovered, then opened. The moth
had shimmering green wings
with a shadowed eye in the shimmering.
It was not a luna moth,
not a butterfly. It opened
wings of feathered beauty, a night sky
full of moon and stars,
a ripple, Nefertiti's dream, a song.
It was magic. I tossed it there,
an embrace, a sliding of fingertips,
an Egyptian memory rippling
though oceans, stopping time.
When I asked, the shimmering wings
opened in front of his eye,
fluttering above the memory
of a cheekbone.
A moth but not a butterfly
tumbling through time. It hovered,
then flew.

Virtuoso

Inspired by the music of Kathleen Ryan

Her music sang from the mountains
and the prairie, magnificent oceans of sky
traveling across the transparent blue of evening
into a virtuoso tumble of falling stars.
Under the constellation of Cassiopeia,
the bray and the rhythm of her donkey,
wildflowers in Colorado, blooming into an Autumn wind,
leaves falling in a light rain,
the colors escaping into a counter-melody.
At the piano, her hands
her ankle-length red dress,
all of the notes sunlit.
"Water in a Dry Land"

We are walking around the reservoir
of the town where we used to live
in Iowa, walking with our memories
through a wide field blooming with sunflowers.
Redwing blackbirds fly from the fence
in waves. In the distance,
an owl, a silo, an old pony.
In the sky, a tiny whir of a bird
golden-crowned kinglet, fast moving, whimsical.
On the branch of a cottonwood tree,
a wood thrush. Music escaping in ripples
from the open top
of the century-old Chickering piano.
"What the Stars Saw on the Prairie."

Night drifts into a photograph,
Sandie with her horse, Lady Cara,
draped with a colorful blanket.
In a deserted ballroom, I'm still waltzing
in the sunflower dress she gave me,
dancing in the arms of an invisible partner,
what I did during those times.

I shiver when I remember the phone call that night.
She was in the passenger seat
when her car slid in front of a Mack truck
on the road to a movie in Ottumwa
on an icy evening.
"Missy Kara Surveys the Pasture, Lays Claim"

All afternoon, the chapel
was draped with Sandie's saris.
I led *kaddish* at her memorial
because I knew Hebrew and could read it with feeling.
I think of her at sunsets, when the colors
intensify, vibrate, layer and disappear.
I feel her dancing inside
the autumn leaves that flare like flames.
The light disappeared slowly that afternoon,
new snow around the chapel,
my prayers, the grand piano, so many memories
before they bulldozed the walls
and the saints in the stained-glass windows.
"A Handfull of Quietness."

A series of tiny melodies,
brief encounters,
written for the left hand.
I love these notes
the way I love my desk,
sunrise and galaxy swirls
in the knotted pine.
The way I love my cello,
as the wood sings and vibrates
rosebuds and butterflies
from the f-holes.

The way I love the feel
of my husband's arms and legs
wrapping around me
as I dream.
"Tangle" "Release" "Bless"
"Love like the Earth."

An improvisation, a cadence of chords
now blended with the antique voice
of a cello. Memory, a hummingbird
threading the branches of a cypress tree
as it stretches away from the western wind,
omen of imminent fog from the Pacific.
An invitation to enter the earth again,
to feel, to see, to love
to dream inside a waterfall of music.
"Blue Paradise"
"Above the Shining Clouds."

Cello Lesson

Down a flight of stairs
on a snowy evening
in Ashland, by Lithia Park.
He's playing Bach
in the cheese shop
as diners finish their brie,
flatbread, soup and wine,
some listening, some not.

We sit on a stone bench,
for this moment
forgetting to order tea
or an oatmeal cookie.
We're here for the music
and when he plays the D-Minor
Bach Sarabande
by memory, with his eyes closed
it opens my heart.

Later, he flies into my dream,
a yellow bird
singing high rippling notes
I can't follow with my cello.

As the full moon shimmers the ocean,
I hear him whisper . . .

Let all technique
fly out the window
into the salty waves
and from your heart
let that beautiful note
fly.

Emotions expand into vibrato,
color and light,
a curtain of blue butterflies.
The first note of the Popper Requiem,
a meteorite
falling into the ocean.

And that perfect note
I so desperately want
and can almost feel in my body,
swimming so deep
inside me . . .

It's something about the heart
breaking open.

Magnificat

For J.S. Bach

It was the old man's 285th birthday –
and I mean the Maestro,
the illuminata, Johann Sebastian Bach.
I was a university student, and to celebrate
three centuries of musical genius,
our conductor led a twenty hour marathon concert
starting early in the morning.
All day, musicians and students migrated
in and out of the auditorium,
with motets, cantatas and concertos.
A bare-footed organist played
the Toccata and Fugue in D Minor,
then a prelude entirely with his feet.
I was amazed at the synergy of dance and sound.

Our concertmaster dazzled us by playing
the Sixth Bach Cello Suite, arranged for violin,
with his eyes closed. No music stand
as he tuned to an inner singing.
Segue to the entire orchestra walking on stage
to play the Second Brandenburg Concerto,
the Concerto for Two Harpsichords,
the Concerto for Three Harpsichords,
and later, just after sunset, the Magnificat.
I was playing cello next to the harpsichord,
inside the sway of its musical body,
surrounded by tones that took me back
to an earlier century.

That night, I had my first experience
of musical transcendence.
The moon was glowing through stained glass.
On the stage, we were playing the Magnificat.
Inside, we were flying in other-worldly ecstasy.

By 10:00 that night, I could swear the Maestro was there,
listening and sometimes playing with us.
Years later, on the other side of the continent,
one of my private pleasures is playing the Bach Cello Suites
late at night, with no one listening.
And sometimes, by the ocean
with the moon glowing towards full,
the old man whispers to me.

Ultra-Body Over the Mountain

So Larry says to the impromptu dancer, *This one is in eleven. I'd like to see what you do with it.* He's playing the silver flute with a trio of jazz musicians at Union Square, high notes fluttering through a curtain of butterflies, musical nectar flying to the Steinway piano and fretless bass. She has already taken over the open space in front of the stage, smiling coyly like a geisha, winking behind her paper umbrella.

The dancer spins out of a time warp, waving peacock feathers. Black slinky pants gyrating like a snake. So thin she does not need her pink leopard bra, so she tosses it to the audience. She whirls like a dervish, a helicopter, a typhoon, her long black hair flying under a straw hat edged with a brown ribbon. The ribbon, the edge of a solar system. Her turquoise glass bead earrings orbiting like planets on a belly dancer's belt. Arc of sun shining on silver, spraying light.

Steinway, flute and bass begin riffing "Ultra-Body Over the Mountain." Larry's tune. The dancer, maybe Japanese, way over the hill. Arms flying, leg kicked over her shoulder. She's a unicorn leaping through time. After the rippling cadences of the flute solo, she knows the applause are for her. She opens her arms to the crowd, blows kisses to the audience.

A homeless man in bright green shorts orbits the square, sweetly happy for these few moments. His hands remember the trumpet he used to play, his childhood friend's conga drum. The bass improvisation is floating into an African dance, tribal rhythms swaying his legs and back. He leaves the lunch someone gave him on the stage. He has to keep dancing. No roof over his memories, an ocean of sky, floating with boat-shaped clouds.

A circular wind from the ocean is spinning across the stage. Green shorts gyrate with tapestry shirt. The Japanese dancer has become a unicorn. She almost smiles. A shower of glass beads reels around her, the planets of a tiny universe, with a meteor shower of silver flute burning a path through the stars. Her stars.

The unicorn spins through time, her long Japanese hair flying in the wind. Almost a pirouette, as much as the concrete will allow. Over the mountain, maybe a moon, maybe a sun. Perhaps a butterfly. The tune climbs the mountain – weaving and winding to its slinky final chord. The butterfly bows, deep diva, face to the floor, arms flying to the moon, to the moon, to the moon.

Earthquake, 5 A.M.

Temblor wakes me with a kiss.
On the other side of the wall,
a whirring of water.
I open thin blinds to calla lilies,
belladonna, the garden of early
morning light.

After the earthquake
the neighborhood dogs howl,
then a silence
that wraps the morning.

Blackbird, Plum, Ripple

As the sun falls into the ocean,
a blackbird
flies across my window.

The plum
hot pink and obsidian
clouds of sunset,
a purple velvet pillow
hanging low on the horizon.
A city of light
incandescent
where the ocean meets
the edge of the continent.

Follow the waves
across a ripple of ocean.
In the sandbox
I dig a hole to China.

In my open palm
I carry a sand dollar into
the maze, the kaleidoscope, the enigma.
A blackbird crosses my shadow,
and the colors multiply.
A shower of falling stars
flying like birds across the sky
and suddenly
the earth is singing.

What Your Cat Did During Your Vacation at the Grand Canyon

I was walking down my very own street when Poppy, the rescue cat who lives next door, attacked a Siberian Husky. She's in the habit of attacking large dogs. Sometimes, she thinks my husband is a large dog.

Before she was rescued, her owner jumped off the Golden Gate Bridge. Full moon, facing the city as he flew.

When Beverly took her home, Poppy was afraid of everything. Now, she is sometimes friendly, but later changes her mind and hisses at tricycles and the mailman. Then she stretches, rolls, and does cat yoga on the sidewalk. Poppy likes to swat butterflies and eat basil leaves from my garden. She is random in her fickleness.

Beverly is riding a mule down a switchback in the Grand Canyon. The Bright Angel Trail. My husband unlocks the door to her duplex, and Poppy meows and purrs before she eats. She has plenty to say until her food dish hits the floor. Content at last, or at least, quiet. A few minutes later, Poppy forgets who he is and attacks him from the balcony.

I wonder what happened during those five days before they found her. And the five days before he jumped. Imaginary mice running across the balcony. Bridges and bones. Daddy howling at the moon. At night, I wonder what she dreams.

Under a Copper Moon

After the storm, a dream buffalo
nested in our yard
surrounded by lavender.

Buffalo clouds
thundering on the horizon.

Clouds like white turtles
crawling across a wide lake of sky,
blue and shimmering.

When a buffalo enters your dream,
listen for arpeggio hooves,
the weight of music,
a copper moon
above a vanishing prairie.

Timpani of thunder pounding red clay,
the weight of time.
The light at the edge of the universe.

Canon for Bears and Ponderosa Pines

Maybe a canon, like bears climbing a mountain,
the impossible note, the way a string vibrates
at the intersection of bow and memory.
A calliope hummingbird
hovering over a branch of hibiscus
before the green wings lift, dive, flit
into the invisible.

The impossible climb, the arpeggio
of a sacred mountain in Nepal
where they don't allow human trekkers.
The color of sky, a single line of pink over silver,
ethereal, flooded with light
before the sun falls into the Dudh Kosi River.

Sometimes, music feels impossible,
something buried so deep inside me
it could take a lifetime
for my fingers to learn
the cello's toning to what I hear.
A canon for bears and ponderosa pines,
a garden of calla lilies unfurling,
a night of peonies, tiny ants
opening trills of blooms.

Impossible, but I try it anyway,
the sun blinding, climbing the Himalayas
over the icefall, the shadow of Dhaulagiri
tumbling down the river, a cascade of minor notes
so sweet, a mountain bird drunk with song,
a snow leopard disappearing behind an avalanche.
The roaring pulls you out of your tent,
out of a dream, into the night
where the music, like a snow leopard
is impossible.

Years ago, I dreamed a four part canon
all night, the voices like honey,
bears climbing a mountain
lit with early morning sun, the ponderosa pines
singing notes on a pipe organ
in a cathedral of trees,
sunlight pouring through the colors
and shape of a high window.

All of the trees in the forest
sang to me that night,
the canon weaving a gentle wind
through the branches. I will never forget the joy
I felt that morning, sun filtering
into a pentagonal room, stained glass windows,
the ocean humming in the distance.

Sometimes, remembering
is a feeling without a form,
the bears scattered into the forest,
their footprints changing shape,
climbing a mountain of melting snow.
Sometimes, the ponderosa pines whisper,
like love, like music. The memory
beyond my fingers.

It is the poem that cannot be written,
the memory of beauty,
the canon, amber light in a cathedral,
the moon rising over a forest of ponderosa pines,
black bears lost in their winter dreams,
the memory of a trout
leaping over white water,
the river singing, the music, suddenly
at the edge of possible.

Igneous

Eat this stone
from the kitchen of the earth
Toss it into the magma
of a volcano

Marinate
the boulder
Slide it into a stone pie
to be baked
in Earth's oven
Doing what it does best

Skip this stone
over a crater lake
water in the mouth
of the igneous
soup

Wear a garnet tie
a ruby ring, shale shoes
a tiara of opals
luminous with dreams

And like a child
humming a stone tune
searching for a path of pebbles
through the geckos, the dinosaurs
in a fairy tale,
put it in your pocket

Walk out of the forest
where rhododendron trees
map hexagons of blossoms
under your footsteps

And let the stone
in your pocket
whisper its secrets
to the moon
to the shower of asteroids
to the singing sky

Jar with Dragons

A walk through the Asian Art Museum in San Francisco

1.
Jar with dragons among clouds.
Ribbons of red and green wind.
Sunflowers blooming out of nowhere
calling me back through time
to an owl, a fish, a woven knot.

2.
Notice the ripples, the sway of the river
how the sun illuminated
a carved boat
on a river without a name.
A silver vessel laden with scrolls,
papyrus inscribed with memories of
love nights under a copper moon,
what the Pharaohs dreamed.

3.
Ashes in a ceremonial urn
surrounded by fossils of shells
that were used as money,
traded for sesame oil, rice and fish.
An enamel box
where pelicans escape
behind centuries of hand-rolled glass.

4.
Bottle with melon-shaped body
and the legs of an elephant.
Bowl with peony and lotus,
orbiting the memory
of a honey-scented wind.
Moonlight scattered through branches
over the koi pond.
A world remembered in porcelain,
topaz blue and ancient light.

5.
Notice the way the dragon appears
out of nowhere.
The girl who will be a geisha
riding the tortoise,
her wings still attached, but transparent.
The lacquered box she holds,
inlaid with mother of pearl,
a secret you are not allowed to enter.

6.
What captured me was simple.
A turquoise sky above the peonies.
Tiny boats like lanterns
floating around an island
of red maple trees.
Full moon above a floating world.

7.
The wood becomes a river,
a galaxy, an eye.
A story told slowly,
through centuries.
By the ocean, the full moon
ripples the water,
Venus and Jupiter still hovering
above the horizon.
The music comes from inside,
but after carving,
the wood remembers how to sing.

Music of the Spheres

My mother is leaning over a concert grand piano, mirrored hands. Her hair in an updo, like Judy Garland, and her voice, a blend of Ella Fitzgerald, Billie Holiday and Danny Kaye. She sings with the musical mahatmas, Count Basie, Duke Ellington and Tommy Dorsey; tossing solos like rings around the moon. They have waited rainy decades to meet again. Humid summers in Harlem floating up to the stratosphere. In the afterlife, they are singing the music of the spheres. Shooting stars, a trajectory of interweaving vectors, voices in perfect harmony. From her voice, a new universe is forming, a tropical paradise, the delicate tumbling light of a new generation of musical journeys. She tells me, "The miracle is the moment."

Photographs of the Pleasure Quarter

The bars across the window say everything,
the way light falls across their shoulders,
cut by shadows. Beautiful women
of the Pleasure Quarter,
walking among images of the floating world.

The courtesan's eyes are shadowed,
inviting but hidden.
Sadness sleeps under the knot
of the obi pulling at her chest
behind the slatted window.

A tightening under her skin
spreads on the calligrapher's scroll.
She whispers to him,
her face beautiful in moonlight.
She pours him a cup of sake,
sweet in a lacquered cup
but keeps her heart in the shadows.

The paintings on her kimonos tell stories,
light escaping
from the scent of cherry blossoms.
The splash of a silver koi
before it disappears.

The shy woman by the window
writes haiku in her pillow book,
a bridge over the koi pond,
nightingales of longing.
Chrysanthemum by her bedside,
her emotions hidden inside the petals.

She dreams of crossing
the great ocean, floating across Hiroshige waves
to the land where the sun
pours lemon light from the East.

Before boarding the boat,
her kimonos tied with a silk rope
in a *furoshiki*,
she steals a final look at the flowering pear trees
by the Kamo River.

Ice Field

*While listening to the San Francisco Symphony
perform "Ice Field" by Henry Dreyfuss Brant*

The ecstatic craziness of Ice Field
echoes through a thunderstorm.
I'm back in time, looking through a screen door in Iowa,
watching hail bounce on the asphalt.
In the morning, ice sheathes the branches
of cottonwood and walnut trees.
Ice jazz, winter birds flying through a snow storm.

It's an echo of Manhattan street noise,
a mirror of the spatial effects of music –
the Cotton Club in Harlem, a saxophone riffing,
the trumpet insisting that body and soul
leap out of the velvet chair
to dance with the crazy man
singing loud and wild
between subway cars of the A Train.

Billie and Ella are wailing
about our crazy planet's hexagonal dreams
narrated by ribbons of timpanis
xylophones, marimbas, floating violins
moments after Romeo drank the poison.
The percussion – rats and cockroaches
scuttling around the rubble of skyscrapers
moments before the last breath of this world.

And then a shaft of light (from God?)
Or a glint of sunlight
reflected from the brass slider
of a trombone wailing on B-flat.
The floating note of God's last dream,
ocean, waves, silence
swallowed by the last green wave (of eternity?)

or was it a whale? A tornado? A musical dream
winding through eighteen brass feet
of a tuba's final long low note?

An atonal pattern shimmies
through a shaman's painted pipe,
the organ's pedal tones rising
out of the earth, like a redwood tree,
a volcano of rumbling
through a scattering of random pipes,
the heaving, smoking remains of an air chest,
a train wreck, a national disaster, low frequency,
off the tracks.

Viewed from the moon
the earth is spinning, the stars turning,
the galaxy whirling in mad pirouette.
Percussion jazz riff of a meteor shower's dream,
or was it a stampede of elephants
pounding red clay?
A high school band warming up
for the halftime of a football game –
trombones blaring black ice,
the padded shoulders of the class hulk
a *mariachi* of drums and marimbas
longing for the prom queen
in a nightmare of a wet dream?

Winter brass, the alarm
in my high school classroom during a bomb scare.
Students streaming out of the doors
to city streets, far away.
Pay attention to the cellist, who went to the music room
to carry the cello she calls "The Rosebud"
out of the building with her.

She hoofs it to 79th Street at Central Park West,
following memories of dinosaur bones,
the fluorescent rocks she saw over and over
at the Museum of Natural History.

Is it music or soundscapes,
rising like a flood?
Or ice wrapping trees
with the memories of our watery planet,
now frozen, now rippled
with an ocean of violins, the clash of percussion
the wildness of winter jazz?
Somewhere, an ice field,
light refracted through a prism
before the blue curtain closes
for the last time, the last breath
of an imploding universe
before it dreams, shatters itself
and is reborn.

ORB

Circular glow
of seven city lights,
above them, full moon.
On the sand dune
fat drops of dew on the ice plants.
Further out, glow of moon
on the water.
Four a.m., must return
to circular dream.

Joy, like a Purple Balloon

for Erik

That morning, a man and his young daughter
were crossing Geary Boulevard
as we waited for the light.
They were both wearing purple
and she was holding three helium balloons
on long strings. Her tiny hands
floating with joy,
the balloons, a kaleidoscope of color.
The two of them
carrying all of the joy
of the human race.
I thought at that moment
if someone from another galaxy
wanted to visit life on this planet,
I would want it to be
right here and right now.
You told me you hoped
that tiny child
would hold tightly to the strings.
And at that moment, I thought
what a miracle, you and I,
among all the humans
on this flying jewel of a planet,
were lucky enough to find each other.
A miracle, a gift –
your heart filling with music,
my heart full with joy.
At our wedding, all around us
friends, family and joy
like a huge bouquet of purple balloons
floating, flapping, flying
in a wild wind.

Best Day Ever

By the Cherry Blossom Sushi Bar,
the sky is full of Japanese kites
fluttering like koi
in the ocean-scented San Francisco wind.
A girl runs down the street
laughing with her father. She's eating
a mango ice cream cone
and wearing a purple sequin sweatshirt
with a message: Best Day Ever!

I think of my father
in a parallel, interpenetrating world.
He loved sashimi
and would have wanted to come with me
today, for lunch and conversation.
I would tell him about playing Beethoven's Ninth Symphony
on the same stand as my husband,
my new novel, narrated by a mermaid,
and finally weeks of open time
to call it into being.
Best Day Ever!

Six years ago in the morning,
my father left this world.
Over time, his memory
became a source of strength to me,
and joy. I would have wanted him
to give me away at our wedding,
but maybe he was doing that
in a parallel, interpenetrating world.
Best Day Ever!

I am left only with today,
another morning of light, a gift
to be in this world, drinking green tea
watching the street parade
through floor to ceiling windows,
then indulging my mile a day walking habit
at the beach, before the wind
picks up from the Pacific.
Tonight, a Solstice Dance. I will wear
velvet, sparkles and lace
when StringFire plays a waltz
called "Solstice Wedding."

City of the Past, City of the Future.
Sunlight filled with joy.
A homeless man by the Symphony
asks if I have brought him a tangerine today.
Yes, three of them, some toothpaste, a fig bar
and a new pair of socks.
I wonder if my father sees me today
or if he is far away.
I wonder what he has learned
in the City of Immortality
and how it will feel to meet him there one day.

Back on Planet Earth,
I walk to the Post Office,
the thrift store, the bagel shop,
the fruit and vegetable stand.
And from that other world,
I hear him whisper,
You were born to live in the City of Joy.
Every day, choose to walk there.
Back at home, rainbow over the ocean,
unexpected light.
Best Day Ever!

Garden Buddha

Halfway around the world,
the first ray of sunlight
opens the eye of the stone Buddha
in the temple garden.

Birds of Paradise
reflecting on the silver
of dew on grass.

At the edge of the enigma,
temple deer wander
through the pink of awakening buds,
chrysanthemums in the garden.

Music of white deer
at the edge of the forest,
the whisper of a fairy tale
in an almost forgotten language.

Somewhere, the moon is shining,
light through branches, a sudden story,
a path through rhododendron trees
with an unexpected ending.

I tumble back through time.

Embraced by Trees

While hiking in Muir Woods

Lichens and gnomes
in the bark of giant redwoods,
ribbons of brown and pink,
striations remembered from earlier times.

Long fingers of ferns, water music,
and above us, stars of light
dazzling through the trees.

On the hiking trail,
a young girl from Tahiti is singing.
She twirls in her red dress,
a full circle around her
tiny thunder thighs.

By the river, a scented eucalyptus wind.
White deer from the albino herd
follow a trail of berries and stones
to the edge of the creek
under the stone bridge.

I embrace the forest,
and the silence I need today
returns to me, inside the bark
of a redwood tree, growing for centuries
inside a cathedral of leaves.

A chord of trees,
the wind full of music,
arms of branches reaching into a tribal memory,
sandals and robes in the holy land,
a dream, my father's blessing.

I still remember his words . . .

*Be at Peace now.
Walk gently through the forest.
Listen to the heartbeat
of the earth.*

Fire Walk

I fall through the ice
where your collarbone cracks.

The deepest wound
is just below the rib
where the breathing stops.

Sheep run down the mountain
in cumulus clouds
that shield
the body of fire
with the mystery of
the dark.

Sun steams rain from the sidewalks
where the edges of oriental poppies
become translucent.

It's all a coded message
a humid afternoon of petals
even if the truth shines only for a nanosecond
before it evaporates again.

Ferry Boat to the Moon

I am the Angel of Death
to the snails in our garden,
as they ride a trumpet leaf to the composter bin,
the shadow over the ants in our sink,
ready to start a flood.
They are swept into arms of sound
and reborn as flowers.

I open my eyes
and I am on a ferry to San Francisco
or maybe Manhattan, a hard rain
patterning the window on the lower deck.
Or maybe it's the window of a space shuttle,
a satellite orbiting the moon
inside the music of the spheres.

In Manhattan, the art professor
is driving a tour bus.
We are on the way to the Cloisters
to get lost inside a bead
with more than 100 tiny carved figures.
We will follow the unicorns
to tapestries of other dimensions.

The music of the spheres
opens passageways to a deeper way of hearing,
waves of interlacing blue light,
time travel to a parallel universe, where
everything floats like the pattern of rain
outside a ferry boat window.

I close my eyes
and awaken inside a forest of birdsong,
a floating raft of infinity
where sound becomes light

and desires become dreams on waves
traveling across the Pacific.

I am the Angel of Transformation
and New Beginnings. In the museum,
tiny carved figures dance out of the bead
and ride the unicorn.
The tour bus becomes a space shuttle.

The snails become fractals
in a painting of calla lilies opening,
a vision of new life.
In Central Park, my memories become butterflies.
Their blue wings fill with light,
and rowboats under the bridge
sparkle silver.

The music knocking on the door
to your heart
is curled inside a conch
on a beach or a tropical island
close to the center of a parallel universe
where sound becomes light
and everything sings.

Catalina Island

I sneeze and the car alarm outside my window intones with long duck sounds. A mallard swims into the dream that tapped me early in the morning, the sun a memory, a glowing tangerine over Catalina Island.

I walked into a shop by the Avalon Theater and found an island skirt with two rows of ruffles, thigh high. We waited for a ride on a boat with a glass bottom, above tropical fish and kelp forests, just in time for the Flying Fish Festival.

In the rickrack of memory, my mother watches a dolphin from the porthole of our cabin on the cruise ship. We are sailing to Mexico. She is still singing to me as stars from a distant universe tap on my window.

Where it Comes From

The Muse is an elephant seal,
swimming in the wake of the Golden Gate Ferry.
The Muse is a snowman
beginning to melt into your imagination,
an exotic bird singing a trill
you heard in a Mozart cantata,
a canon for bears and ponderosa pines.
The Muse is in bed with you
when you wake up in the morning.
She was reading fortune cookies all night
below a copper moon.
The Muse is a thin line on the horizon
just before dawn,
as the light is coming back.
The Muse is a powder blue Fiat
having wild electric dreams,
a thunderstorm on the prairie,
a flash of lightning flying by your window.
The Muse is an extraterrestrial,
silver in your dreams,
whispering secrets of other worlds.
The Muse is a goat,
born a few hours ago, in Iowa or Nepal,
in your arms now
because it smells like new hay.

Intermezzo

For Pyotr Ilyich Tchaikovsky

He wrote it for the violinist
with a firebird on his tie –
the dancer from the Russian
ballet. He believed in beauty.
By the 20th century, the beautiful
music had all been written,
so they went for ugly –
tempest, wind and rain.

What about French
kisses, a refuge of comfort
in a war-torn night?
What about strawberry
sorbet from his favorite ice cream shop
in Paris, around the corner
from the Russian composer?

Love is translation – Swan Lake,
The Nutcracker, Sleeping Beauty.
But life is a series of triangulars
with adagio honey in between.
The musician swims with the dancer.
The dancer longs for the firebird.
A long, flying leap
keeps his heart from floating away.

Picasso's Dream

On a blue evening,
he played a blue guitar
as the rain whispered
a blue song.

Above him, a sky of silver stars
collected the music of a cobalt night.
Silver words, an ascending arc
of sky arpeggios.

All night long he sang
in the shadow of silver dreams.
Henna constellations, the amber light
of a cubist supernova,
exploding all he knew.

In the morning, silver memories
gathered from blue shadows
released into the light.

Pentagram: Garden Walk

1.

Glass sculptures in a sidewalk garden
at the edge of the succulent museum,
exotic cactus blooming
above fjords of underwater dreams
revealing their names in mysterious voices.
Purple petaled anemones, birds of paradise,
clusters of California poppies.
The purple flowering cactus, a grandfather
homesteading, glazed and dreaming
for a hundred years.

2.

My mother's garden had tea roses,
a delicate pink,
with irises and tiger lilies in the back yard.
One year she grew tomatoes,
string beans, cucumbers, and five kinds of lettuce.
On the other side of the continent,
I am dreaming of yellow irises,
intoxicated with the wild
perfume of alyssum fields.
My mother's voice tumbles through time
with a bumblebee and a green feather.

3.

The rose whispered pink as the moon was rising.
I carried her to the terra cotta garden,
cradled in moonlight, cradled in my arms.
All night in my dreams,
a tornado in slow motion

with petals scenting a wild wind
I could dance to –
a vision of slanted light,
an ancient promise.

4.

That night, as I was dreaming, cactus
rose petals and sand washed glass
speaking in a language
I couldn't remember in the morning.
My emotions on a high trapeze,
caught in the netting of a six-year-old ballerina's
tutu. All night long,
my memories hiking through calla lilies,
succulents and birds of paradise.

5.

Love is a whir of hummingbirds,
an open window,
a garden of passion flowers and wild orchids,
indigo butterflies mating in a kaleidoscope of wings,
a memory, a dream you suddenly remember.
All night, a kaleidoscope of pink roses,
the scent of eucalyptus,
the quiet whisper of a hidden world
that has always known your name.

Transmigration

The window washer should be in a Yiddish folk tale. Sholom Aleichem would call him *Shmoozitz, Menachem* or *Schmendel*. His head appears at my window whenever I am trying to change my clothes or think. His ladder is patched with bird droppings and paint chips, a fragment of color from a painting in a dream.

My thoughts are climbing emerald stems. A beanstalk, the corona of a sunflower, that certain shade of blue after the sunrise. I remember the ruby necklace my Grandmother wore. I wonder what my Grandfather whispered to her in the moonlight. Maybe a ladder to an unfinished dream.

The dream is a window in a Yiddish folk tale. Everyone builds a raft called *Noah's Ark,* with split timber cabins above the raft and open windows. The women dress themselves in rainbows. They sail together into a new world.

The Open Book of Riddles

I can disappear for you.

I dance with you
then vanish into the steam
of Kabuki gardens
or the path by the Kamo River
over the Shoji Bridge
to the Gion Shrine.

In the early afternoon
we spin like tea leaves
inside a jade cup.
Then I am lost inside
a herd of heifers
grazing in the snow.

We invent a story,
the open book of riddles.
I see them in your face
but nobody can read the mirror.

You call me Snow Princess,
braid my hair.

You catch the snowfall
on your fingertips.
You can trace the pattern
in ice crystals, but they melt
dancing to your arm.

In a redwood forest
I fall to you
like a snowflake on your eyelash,
caught for a moment
then melted to body heat.

Now you see it. Now you don't.

KALEIDOSCOPE

A tree grew out of a lie
        on the dance floor
under old growth pine
   with stellar jays hidden in the branches.

Your body unlocked a long river,
        arms and legs unraveling
   inside a koan of song,
        moonlight through branches.

A branch grew out of a note
        in a minor key
   the notes round like apples or the moon,
        waiting to be written.

An apple grew out of a dream,
        sweet and full of poison.
   Light traveling on the ecliptic
        beyond the moon.

She thought she saw a planet
        through the narrow end of a telescope
   but the meadowlarks kept singing
        outside her window.

In this way, her heart became
        a kaleidoscope,
   a planet, the scent of jasmine,
        a silent song, maybe a symphony,
   ice rings around the moon.

October Secret

You were the last survivor
of the North American Cloud People,
their tribal stories a memory –
three million shards of glass
surfing with the sharks at Half Moon Bay.
Your parents' fantasies,
all of their secret hopes for you
over the waterfall.

You were the belly dancer
whose hips etched a silver cloud
backlit by the moon.
You rippled the ocean
with salty light, as your thighs became
hills blooming with marigolds.

Scholars and art historians
tried to understand you, but
the mystery could not be penetrated
with the mind alone.
The Italian sculptor, his head a bouquet
of dark angel curls,
waited for you in a tide of salty dreams.

Centuries later, a man with wide cheekbones
asks you to dance on a sprung wood floor.
He covers you with feathers.
He considers you for a sculpture
in his erotic book of dreams.

That night, empty directions in every room.
Paint from your dream vacation
inside a puddle of turpentine.
Light inside a cloud
rippling to the edges of the universe.
Yesterday's full moon eclipse
hovering over a waterfall of fog.

A Ruby in his Beard

His face was a Russian novel, and the clue was in his beard. A flame, a ruby, a tear. A shard of light from an older story, hidden in his heart, embedded in his face. Clues appeared in mirrors, the afterglow of love nights, flames and burning cities. The road by the farmhouse where he hid, then wandered into the future or the past.

Life became a meteor shower, a deck of cards, a dart game on the wall of a country inn. A river of expectations, changing as the sun skidded across a sky full of cumulus clouds and thunder. Mirrors appeared and disappeared in dance halls, stone mansions, what he saw by the side of the barn when he was eight years old. A left turn into joy or sorrow, a ride on the wings of a snowy owl. A message from an unexpected snowstorm.

When I told him about the novel, he asked about the ending. No flames in the copper shadow of the moon. Every year, the light returns. The sun floating like a swan on the river. The stone well by the farmhouse filling with water. After the ice cracks, his heart begins to speak again. In April, a goose shadow flying across the moon. The fortune cookie says, "I believe in happy endings."

While Listening to the Quartet for Piano and Strings by Tom Darter

"Movements are played without pause." ~ Tom Darter

Snow tumble
or maybe notes
falling from metallic sky
counting breaths
between allegro and adagio.
Drunk cumulus
on a pizzicato horizon.
Pointillistic rain
walking up the fingerboard,
darting into silver puddles reflecting
nimbus clouds at the center of
Rorschach ripples.
Musical hands kneading bread
at the edge of time.

Only the cellist knows for sure
where the melody tumbles
into a flood
of grasshoppers,
or a slow cadenza
where the singularity of a black hole
unblocks the spacetime continuum
and unravels like a river
full of spawning salmon
swimming upstream
as white water tumbles down a mountain.

The pianist dreams with his hands,
ascending a spiral of notes and stars,
into a river of unexpected tenderness.
Night is a tiny blue frog
leaping through time
and all seven layers
of the human soul.

As the canyon fills with light
and sound, illuminating the cave paintings
of a shaman artist, centuries ago
or maybe the future,
the sun rises over a cadenza.
A single leaf, red at the edges.

A katydid, what you heard
on the porch last night,
when all you wished for
tumbled into a primal silence
instead of a bright star.

Now, the rocking ocean.
Now, wave after wave of
thunder, passion, tenderness,
light from an earlier millennium
traveling to this moment.
Suddenly, a line of crazed gerbils
skittering through the Steinway
and the singularity of time.

I remember what he whispered,
what he sang,
the full weight of his body
rising and falling, an ocean,
a moon, a supernova,
arms suspended over the black notes
and the ivory,
all of his fingers dreaming
before he flew.

Moon Blizzard, Saxophone Dream

In Iowa, the memory of an ice storm,
   early daffodils freezing under the thunder blizzard.
Olive and walnut trees bent to the ground
      glittering in the early morning sunlight.

   Raven on the rooftop. Cacophonous song.
The woman in my dream, arching her back
   like my younger self. A willow,
      a salty moon.

Somewhere, a starfish under blue waves,
   dreaming of kelp forests.
Somewhere, a pelican dreaming of coastal trees,
      maybe cedar, maybe San Francisco.
A long train in the distance, saxophone on the tracks,
   wailing an Fm^7 chord.

Now, a flock of wild parrots
   in the trees by Telegraph Hill.
Jazz riffing the sunset over rippled water,
      a silver line of light at the end of the sky.
Dreams full of wings
   reflected on night waves,
a salty tune, migrating to the left coast.

Sky full of music, a nighthawk,
      a saxophone riff of falling stars.
Suddenly, I am smiling
   like that silly sliver of a moon
hovering above the Pacific coast,
      a winter meditation in the waves
   beyond my window.

In the morning, a rainbow, a prayer,
    a flock of parrots, a new beginning
a tree house, a salty song.

Packing Up George

He was a knight on a shining horse,
defender of the downtrodden.

He held the Quixote sword for so many –
a welder burned in an industrial fire,
a recycler whose back was injured
under a ton of bottles, boxes and aluminum cans.
Friends from the Olympic Club
and their auto accidents
as they became longer in the tooth
and longer in the speed of their reaction time.
The artist he helped *pro bono*
to free herself from a credit card scam,
and his friend from the Catholic high school
who was molested by a priest.

George wrote to the Archbishop about that one,
told him, *this has to stop*
if you want to see my donation again.

I remember the attorney down the hall
we called *thunder lizard,*
a pit bull in the courtroom
who could not release the growl
in the rest of his life.
George was the only one in the office
who was not afraid to stand up to him.

He had a discerning eye for people
like what grows wild in your garden –
which weeds to pull
and which seedlings will bloom into flowers.
Each year, he gave a scholarship to a student
from St. Mary's High School –
usually an athlete with promise.

And now,
retirement forced by a huge rent increase.
No, George was not a bottom line man.
He was a knight on a wildcard horse,
with a habit, through the years,
of hiring poets and musicians
who needed an income and insurance.

Today, I'm packing up George,
helping him decide what to keep,
what to shred,
and what to put in the recycle toter.
Keep the California Bar Association card,
the entry card to Mills Law Library.
Keep the Oxford dictionary,
the tomes on elder abuse
worker's compensation appeals
and tenant's rights.
Shred the storage files
from the earlier years of the new century.

No, packing is not as painful,
when you're doing it for someone else,
but to see an entire career dismantled in a week
is something amazing to behold.

George, I hope you enjoy your free time,
get to see a bit more of the world with your wife
visit with your daughters in Hawaii, Colorado and Mexico
and spend more time with your grandchildren.
Treat yourself to a few extra flights
to Chicago and Atlanta with your buddies
to see football games.
I won't wish you more time on the handball court
of the Olympic Club,
because you're already doing that.

And some quiet evening
in front of a fire
with flames like wishes
galloping off on a lucky horse,
or perhaps on a sun-dappled afternoon
while walking towards the
ninth hole on the golf course,
think about all the people you've helped,
all of the lives you have changed
for the better,
and all of the people who bless you.

Six Months in Arosa

The photographs are gone,
but I still remember birds flying to my hand,
squirrels eating hazelnuts from my fingers,
and Sunday morning bells that echoed through the valley.
The Alpine houses in Switzerland
had gardens of wildflowers,
and they told us the milk was so sweet
because the cows ate flowers.

On Thursdays, we hiked further up the mountain
to a tiny church in a pasture,
or sometimes down to the village
for chocolate.
An old man swept the hiking paths
with a straw broom,
and the nuns taught us the few words we knew
of Swiss German.

We were high enough in the Alps
that it snowed twice that summer.
I was learning to be a meditation teacher,
and our guru descended from a helicopter
every few weeks
to bless us and answer questions.

Every morning, fresh bread and sweet butter
on the table. Long meditations
and early morning, as dawn was breaking
and the mountains began to sing,
visions of other worlds revealed themselves.

In October, after the snow came for real,
I took the train to Chur,
speeding down the mountain
through an amazement of branches

and snow. I knit a scarf
that wrapped around my head three times,
and rainbowed to my knees.

As I was hiking, the moonstone I wore every day
fell into the snow,
along with a tiny lacquered photograph of my guru,
maybe an omen
of a very independent soul.
But something deep and silent
extended like moonlight through the mountain,
and wove through my heart and mind,
my dreams and my bones. My memories,
a thousand cows clanging their bells
in the early morning.

When you fly . . .

Things that might be a bomb . . .
Yogurt, avocados, lemonade, iced tea
the endpin of a cello

A banjo, a violin
electronic equipment wrapped carefully
in cotton fabric and bubble wrap
so it won't be damaged after landing

The Empire State Building
The Golden Gate Bridge
The packing cases of the San Francisco Symphony
The Eiffel Tower
The Pyramids at Giza

The unwritten pages of a novel
in the genre of magical realism
An architectural drawing
An algorithm, a vector
An illuminated medieval book of hours
My grandmother's wedding ring

And to the TSA agent
who groped me during the pat down
and then asked me out to lunch . . .

It's not a hand grenade;
it's an avocado.

Zoo Story

12	has a temper tantrum
84	is searching for the fountain of forgetting
17	has a spandex leotard in his dream
22	zebras leap out of their cages
5	his smile leaps onto five different faces
18	patterns of weaving a universe
100	until it all disappears
6	swallowed back
5	into the big bang.
24	nightingales outside the prison wall
1	birdman
32	taking literacy courses
302	studying for the G.E.D.
	at San Quentin
64	writing a poem with
8	seagulls
7	until they fly
6	to Angel Island
5	beyond the stone gray horizon.
108	at this moment
42	the spacetime continuum
17	of a high slate wall
2	without the crayon dream
1	of a solitary seagull
0	floating on the water
	lifting, like the first stage of a rocket,
	to the pock-marked moon.

Hemiola

My mother's spirit appears as a white bird.
Old music on a scratchy phonograph.

Hemiola – a three against two rhythm
from medieval times, music between the lines.

In a garden of white lilies
all night, it feels like walking on the moon.

On a path to nowhere,
a calla lily, a hummingbird, a whir of grasshoppers.

My father was writing a book
before he died.

He gave my mother a dogwood tree,
a symphony of branches.

Weaving through music,
the way a tree grows.

Interrupted, they say, but it feels
like walking on the moon.

Twin Dreams

In my dream, I'm hauling my cello
up Mt. Everest.
I've hired a guide and a Sherpa,
and we're getting ready to climb.
I want to play music on a Himalayan peak
with the sun shining on *mani* stones
and mica. Long low notes
pulsing like a heartbeat in the mountains
with the moon shining
on the Kali Gandhaki River.

In his dream, we are driving in the mountains
in a red Maserati, with gold-flecked metallic paint.
We are going somewhere. Anywhere.
We pass a purple dump truck
a few exits past Mt. Shasta.
He points and says,
"Check out those wheels!
They are large and chrome,
but who puts Infiniti rims on a dump truck?"

The dump truck curves
onto the exit ramp, and we follow.
At the stoplight, we can clearly see
"Infiniti" etched into the chrome
on each of the spokes.
The pattern is like a mandala
in a Tibetan Temple.
In my dream, the monks are chanting
a three day *puja* to the Green Tara.
I follow the cadence of their voices
with my cello, adding a river
of long low notes.

In the shadow of Mt. Shasta,
the dump truck driver pulls into the parking lot
of a fruit and vegetable stand, and we follow.
He buys a bag of oranges.
His shopping cart has Infiniti wheels.
Who would have thought . . .

In my dream, the cello
reappears in a field of sunflowers
with a clear view of Mt. Shasta.
A black bear walks across the road
before he climbs higher up the mountain.
In his dream, the driver is peeling an orange.
He's standing by a silver Honda CRX,
packing his dump truck, piece by piece,
into the hatch.
Infinity packed into a point,
and the driver nods to the silver.
"Everything's in there. It folds up nicely."

Infinite like a mandala
in a Tibetan temple.
Infinite like the eyes
of a thousand Buddhas.
Infinite like the hunger
of a black bear.

At the truck stop, the driver is giving oranges
to his daughters – all twelve of them.
They're wearing tight red sweaters
and low cut jeans, revealing infinity tattoos.
In my dream, the monks
are wearing cinnamon robes.
I bring a bowl of oranges to the monastery kitchen.

In the shadow of Mt. Shasta,
one of the daughters pulls up her sweater
to show my husband the rest of her tattoo.
Infinity collapses into the light,
tricking the bears into thinking it is night.
Halfway around the world
the monks are chanting Tibetan mantras,
but one of the monks is daydreaming
about a Maserati. In the distance, the rush
of the Kali Gandhaki River,
a leap of the imagination, a long surprise
where the laughing music of the water tells us
infinity has a thousand names.

After the End of the Road

I'm driving a Ford Fairlane station wagon,
classic two-tone paint, creamy white
with a thin red stripe on each side.
I'm in New Jersey, driving west to visit Dad and Edie.
They're living in a new house on a new road.
I've been there once before,
but I don't know the exit from Route 78.

I need to call him,
but I don't have his telephone number in the afterlife.
I stop at a little diner in Chatham,
chrome with pink neon lighting the windows,
a Mom and Pop eatery. No telephone booth
but she offers to let me use her phone,
a black rotary model to match the decor.

I empty my purse, full of messages
on tiny scraps of paper
but still can't find his telephone number.
I decide to get back on the road and wing it,
driving through the small towns of my history –
past antique shops, a cannon from the Revolutionary War,
a cemetery lined with flags,
and the ice cream shop
where I went with my girlfriends in high school
to meet boys from other towns.

Somehow, I arrive at their house.
Edie has made an Italian dinner with prawns,
linguini and stuffed artichokes,
which she serves with heirloom silver
over her favorite lace tablecloth.
It's warm and comforting to sit at her table.
A fire is burning. We watch the flames,
warm and comforting, like her heart.

After dinner, my father gives me a compass and a telescope.
Good to find your direction, he says,
among the stars in the dark night.
He tells me, *Always be patient with your husband*
and enjoy the years you have together.
He opens a bottle of Chianti, imported from Tuscany,
and repeats his favorite toast,
May you be as happy as we are!

Tonight in San Francisco, goat cheese ravioli
with roasted red peppers, onions and zucchini
in marinara sauce with basil from our garden.
Soapy water in the sink, comforting me, warming my hands.
It won't always be that way
when I'm living in the stars.

Hidden Variables

*While listening to "Hidden Variables" by Colin Matthews,
performed by the London Philharmonic*

The music felt like a noisy machine.
Rhythmic with a few brief musical interludes
before the skyscraper fell.
The bombing, clearly an inside job.

What I heard . . .
Oboes and bassoons colliding
inside a dream of the human body.
Timpanis, veins and arteries, the rhythm of a heartbeat.
But frozen, an air raid,
a disturbing dream, warped through time.
Everyone in the school hiding under their desks
with coats over their heads.
As if that would help. Or maybe a group of friends
knitting in the dark in the London Underground
during a *blitzkrieg*.

Suddenly, a deconstruction of harmony and time.
Space travel at warp speed,
looking back at the earth from an unknown future.
Intergalactic sky, over the stereotype of a spy movie,
black and white trench coats
colliding on the pages of *Mad Magazine*.

And now, dinosaurs in a cave under
a forest of stalactites.
Lichens and tropical trees before the ice age.
Prehistoric memory.
Tyrannosaurus Rex pounding the earth
before the big freeze,
atonal eruption of volcanos.
Cave men dreaming of cypress trees
in the new millennium.

Centuries later, I sit wondering
what was crushed under the pounding
of that giant dinosaur foot.
Maybe the skeleton of a trilobite?
Perhaps a tiny yellow flower?

A few seconds of musical grace.
Spacetime travel into an amphitheater,
a future a dinosaur couldn't imagine,
and it's peaceful here.
An afternoon by the left coast,
many hours in the garden,
planting bulbs that will grow into purple muscari
and a different kind of music.
Listening, I am a willing servant of beauty,
as I sit here pulling weeds, enjoying the sunshine.
Now, the sun is setting over the Pacific.
Silver waves. A bit of calm.
A cello, a flute, a line of tangerine
at the edge of the sky.

Ode to New Music

Whale swimming through ink.
Slide into third base, underwater.
Home? Vacation? Cage?

Gorillas emerge from low notes on the bass,
backlit by erotic dreams
and the gentle flowing of a harp,
a cricket's song leaping over a waterfall.

I write these notes
to fill my mind
where music doesn't satisfy.

But trapped in a silver room
where time is a banana slug,
time moves slowly.

Miso Soup

In a Japanese raku bowl,
the outline of a face
with green onion hair.

In the temple garden,
a pear branch, a koi pond
below a wooden bridge
arcing to earlier times.

Reflected in steaming water
a memory of Kyoto,
the Golden Pagoda,
a shower of tofu cherry blossoms.

Puberty

She's decided to bind her breasts
but she doesn't know what to do about her hips.
In the bathtub, she still looks like a girl,
her eyes resting on the soft curves of her arms
folded around her shoulders.
Her body, day by day, against her will,
growing more and more lovely
like the calla lilies in her yard.

Her mother calls the school psychologist,
takes long meditative walks at the ocean
to breathe the salty air
and watch the crashing waves.
*Becoming a woman is not
supposed to be this painful.*

"I want to be androgynous," she says,
eating a mango from a bowl
she glazed midnight blue –
her mood each morning before she goes to school.
Her emotions scrape against the world she finds –
poison oak, prickly pear.

She tells everyone who will hear
she is dating her best friend,
until the taunting from classmates follows her home.
Her friend is a Russian beauty;
she praises her mind, her eyes, her beautiful hair.
They both see dragons and hear them
whisper a secret language.

In the attic, sunlight streams across her breasts
through an open window. She stretches
catlike across yellow satin sheets,
her reflection rippled in the mirror

her grandmother brought from Hungary.
She paints herself blue,
a sleeping dragon
stretching across the flat of her belly,
tiny shells ornamenting her arms and toes.

Outside, in the garden
a thin blue waterfall ripples against the green
stems of emerging roses.
If she had the power, she'd will them
to stop growing. A Labrador Retriever
circles the yard and returns to lick her hand,
then runs into a swarm of pink peonies.
A line of tiny ants forces them open.

Her inner garden is darker.
In the distance, a train
emerging from tunnel to night.
At the beach with her lover, a sickle moon
whispers a secret language.
She'd like to paint the rest of her life
in a private universe
only a dragon would understand.

Invisible Ink Picnic

Uranus is a street in San Francisco,
a left turn from 17th Street, close to Mars.
Directions are written in invisible ink
above the Castro District.
Desire on a road tour,
a motorcycle on winding original hills,
streets and alleys, chutes and ladders
weaving up to Twin Peaks.

After the Pride Parade,
six million plastic mannequins
paint an invisible ink picnic.
They feed strawberries
to the cheerleaders of permission
in drag, with pom-poms
and a solar system
of red sequins.

In your kitchen, all of the food is spiced
with erotic fantasies –
a thunderstorm in July,
a memory of Asbury Park
and cotton candy
blowing in the salty sea wind.
Your first kiss under the boardwalk
and what you dreamed that night.

Years later, desire migrated to the Left Coast,
a flaming paper paradise,
thunder over the redwood deck,
the yowling of cats and dogs
while the earth shakes.
Your avocados in terra cotta pots
vibrating like planets, and then
a midnight picnic with all of your closest friends,

feasting on wine, cheese and
gender-changing soufflé.

Admit it, you're spying on your neighbors
with the telescope from your childhood, the one you kept
for so many years,
revealing a copper moon
closer in now, like the fantasies
that rode in your back pocket
and blew open like a bouquet of balloons
on the flagpole of your wildest
erotic dreams, revealed each night on the patio
in invisible ink.

Asphalt Impressionism

Rivulets of yesterday's rain
flow between tiny stones.
Urban artists, chalking murals
to be erased by the next storm.
Floating chaos and trouble in the sky.

Hostage at the 7-11
in flamenco dress with castanets,
floating popsicles of heartache
in the parking lot.

Half a mile to the North,
Bay to Breakers impressionists
wearing rainbow tutus,
followed by a nude brigade of joggers
avoiding chaos in the mirror.

In my world,
bumblebee on a balloon
waiting to pierce your version
of reality.

Owl, Dream, Mountain

I walk into a snowy owl's dream,
a gardenia,
an echo of white roses.
I ride the wide green back
of a turtle swimming underwater.

In the eye of the Buddha,
a pink feather, a blue dream,
the diamond of illumination.
A white owl lifting at sunset,
a whir of feathers. Night music,
a vision on the mountain
shaped like a sleeping princess.

Suddenly interrupted,
the illusion of the world.
Fellow pilgrims on the quest for illumination
climbing Mt. Tamalpais. On the trail
the faint odor of *eau de skunk*.
Raccoons, those bandits of equanimity,
snorfling around the eucalyptus.

At dawn, a dragonfly
hovers over a field of tiger lilies,
the scent of wild orchids, the fire of opium poppies.
In that boulder, halfway up the mountain,
the history of the earth,
everything the owl knows
wanting to fly.

Sunset over the Pacific

for Cassandra

The earth remembers her –
wide stripes of color across the sky,
the sunset singing.
The cobalt blue of the stellar jay
departed for other eyes.
The purple of an amethyst
or the sky?

She is climbing a redwood tree.
She is singing inside a rainbow,
the violet ray dancing through
the light inside of things.
Frog, begonia, lark,
swallowtail
butterfly.

Now, she is everywhere –
the undulation of a snake,
cliffs above the ocean, rippling
pink, lavender and silver.
A sine wave leaning into
the geodesic of time,
the migration of wild geese,
a singularity, where the world is
ending or beginning.

Planting Tulips

Love is a ballerina in an empty field
   planting tulips under a full moon,
      bare feet on black dirt.
Perhaps in two days, maybe three,
   a sky of meteor showers.
      Must be observed in the cricket hours
after the moon falls below
   the sunflower fields.

In her mind, an empty dance floor,
   the invisible partner she will meet
      after the tulips
circle around the sun –
   an orbit of hidden desire
so many times, so many times.

Can you see it from the moon?
   She stopped trying to remember.
      Tulips, crickets, meteor showers.
She watched dragonflies mating
   in a forest of eucalyptus trees.
      A rainbow through a spray of light.
The dream dissolved before a candle
   etched leaf shadows on his shoulders.

Halfway around the world,
   he walks out of a pyramid.
He will follow a thread of light,
   a thread of music,
      the scent of tulips,
bare feet on black dirt
      until he finds her.

Morning Meditation

Once again I am in the silent place
   where all motion is
      sun, moon, universe;
where the tadpole becomes a galaxy
   and stardust is the seed
      of a new life;
where my deepest thoughts and dreams
   sing mountains into being
      sing the moon
and the reflection of junipers
   on the water
      in the hallow carved
   by a shower of falling stars.

I am wide awake
   inside the light that knows my name,
      your name
and the secret silent names
   of lichen, peony, salamander
crossing the mountain path
   and disappearing into ferns and forest,
the underbelly of the dreams
   the planet has been spinning
      for billions of years.

I sing where the light shines
   inside rocks, the song of silver,
the music that becomes clay, mountain, river,
   the cedars along the cliff by the ocean,
      the monarch butterfly, the hummingbird, backlit
         with moonlight, earth and sky.
A billion years, a moment,
      music of touching in the glow of
the peach light of a new morning.

The inner circle
    of the heart inside the heart
where love is an open sky,
    and I follow.

Two Sunsets

This is what you remember . . .
A campfire by the river,
flames reflected on the water.
Silver waves, a rock ledge over the cove,
more than one hundred girls
singing at sunset. The hidden place
where the tadpoles swam with silver minnows,
dragonflies skimming the water.

That summer was the first time
you paddled the green canoe on Lake Cohasset.
You practiced strokes on the dock,
then in deep water. Beyond the edge of the lake,
shadows moving like animals
through the pine forests, a warm wind whistling
through summer on Bear Mountain.

Flying over it now,
the shadow of the plane on the mountain,
the twangy notes of a hammered dulcimer,
a banjo, the low notes of a string bass,
whir into a harmony
that awakens chords
in the place inside you that hums,
where music is born.

In memory, your first airplane flight,
nose to the window
and the wings the stewardess pinned
on your velvet dress.
The sun was setting in the early evening,
and higher, above the clouds,
you watched it set a second time.

Memory spins into music,
a needle on an old Victrola.
Men in tuxedos, women in ball gowns
waltzing on the dance floor,
wood polished to a moonlit shine.
The music, fire by the river,
takes you back in time.

Memory is a tiny frog in your cup,
the rock you used to climb
at the edge of the forest
when you wanted to dream about the future.
In the distance, a fiddle tune
climbing trails on Bear Mountain.

Chords are spreading their fingers like ferns
under old growth pines.
Two sunsets inside the waltz –
a melody that came to you
before the first light of morning.
The notes, low and deep as the earth
a black bear searching for berries,
dreaming of honeycomb,
eating the enigma of mountain light.

Jumping A Train

His name is Luke and he lives in Ohio, fields of wheat, gold and flat in every direction. The way he'd like his mind to become, opium poppies waving in a hot summer wind. Dorothy and the Wizard of Oz.

Actually, his name is Jacob. He ran off with his wife's sister and then decided he didn't like her any better. He escaped both of them by jumping a train to Pennsylvania, leaving a trail of debt in an unmarked mailbox. It was the height of the Great Depression, and the two sisters were forced to raise their children in the same house. They didn't speak to one another, but their children became best friends, riding a single sled down snowy hills in the winter, tossing stones at terra cotta pipes until they broke open. My Grandmother made peanut butter sandwiches for the hobos who knocked at the back door.

Actually, his name is Raphael. His wife threw him out of the house after she read his diary. During my cello lessons, she always brought him a cup of tea. I wanted to tell her, "Leave him alone now. This is my time." But that was after she read his diary. He tells me his son has a lusting for musical instruments. Raphael jumped a train to the edge of the continent, and now he plays cello in Lithia Park for tourists who come to the Oregon Shakespeare Festival. Small girls bring him yellow balloons.

Actually, his name is Tim. His mother lights candles in a French church in New Orleans, and around her, the waters rise. That was before his lungs filled with water. When he was nineteen years old, Tim jumped a train heading north and jumped off in a wheat field. Now, he leaps into your imagination, inventing the life he was not allowed to continue. He sleeps in a cabin filled with candles, toy trains, and beautiful women who want to please him. The afterlife is a magic theatre. He's on a beach covered with chocolate fondue, the waves shimmering turquoise in the distance. A mermaid is feeding him mangoes and papayas from a silver spoon. She whispers a secret before she jumps back into the water.

He walks with the Village Explainer for forty years, until his beard is long and white, until he is the only one who remembers.

About the Author

Diane Frank is an award-winning poet and a cellist in the Golden Gate Symphony. Her friends describe her as a harem of seven women in one very small body. She lives in San Francisco, where she dances, plays cello, and creates her life as an art form. Diane teaches at San Francisco State University and Dominican University. She leads workshops for young writers as a Poet in the School and directs the Blue Light Press Online Poetry Workshop. *Blackberries in the Dream House,* her first novel, won the Chelson Award for Fiction and was nominated for the Pulitzer Prize. She is editor of the bestselling anthology, *River of Earth and Sky: Poems for the 21st Century.*

To schedule readings, book signings and workshops, and to invite her to speak to your book club, contact:

E-mail: GeishaPoet@aol.com
Website: www.dianefrank.net

BOOKS BY DIANE FRANK

Canon for Bears and Ponderosa Pines
Yoga of the Impossible
Blackberries in the Dream House
River of Earth and Sky: Poems for the Twenty-First Century
Swan Light
Entering the Word Temple
The Winter Life of Shooting Stars
The All Night Yemenite Café
Rhododendron Shedding Its Skin
Isis: Poems by Diane Frank

Glass Lyre Press

exceptional works to replenish the spirit

Glass Lyre Press is an independent literary publisher interested in technically accomplished, stylistically distinct, and original work. Glass Lyre seeks diverse writers that possess a dynamic aesthetic and an ability to emotionally and intellectually engage a wide audience of readers.

Glass Lyre's vision is to connect the world through language and art. We hope to expand the scope of poetry and short fiction for the general reader through exceptionally well-written books, which evoke emotion, provide insight, and resonate with the human spirit.

Poetry Collections
Poetry Chapbooks
Select Short & Flash Fiction
Anthologies

www.GlassLyrePress.com

www.ingramcontent.com/pod-product-compliance
Lightning Source LLC
Chambersburg PA
CBHW021445080526
44588CB00009B/693